The Fabulous Fox

an anthology of fact & fiction

The Fabulous

Fox

by Johanna Johnston

illustrated with photographs & prints

Dodd, Mead & Company

New York

Special acknowledgment is made to my daughter,
Abigail Johnston, for her helpful research.

Illustrations in this book are used through the courtesy of: The American
Museum of Natural History, 23, 25; Library of Congress, 66; The Metropolitan
Museum of Art, 53, 55, 56; National Audubon Society, 27; The New York Public
Library, 5, 35, 40, 46; U.S. Fish and Wildlife Service, 10, 11, 12, 21.

The selection on page 30 is from *Beyond Your Doorstep: A Handbook to the
Country*, by Hal Borland. Copyright © 1962 by Hal Borland. Reprinted by permission of Alfred A. Knopf, Inc. The story on page 68, "The Feast for the Fox,"
is from *The Fables of India* by Joseph Gaer. Copyright 1955 by Joseph Gaer.
Reprinted by permission of Little, Brown and Co.

1 2 3 4 5 6 7 8 9 10

Library of Congress Cataloging in Publication Data

Main entry under title:

The Fabulous fox.

   Includes index.
   SUMMARY: An anthology of stories, legends, folk
songs, adages, quotations, and general information
about the fox.
   1.   Foxes—Juvenile literature.   2.   Foxes
(in religion, folk-lore, etc.) —Juvenile literature.
[1.   Foxes (in religion, folklore, etc)]
I.   Johnston, Johanna.
QL737.C22F32   599'.74442   78-21031
ISBN 0-396-07652-1

Contents

The Sly Fox

T HE fox has a reputation all his own. He is the sly one, the cunning one.

Through the centuries, he has been slipping in and out of people's lives. Golden-red, gray, black, or white, he darts in from his wild haunts to upset the arrangements of farmers, gardeners, and other settled folk. Then he streaks away again, to lead anyone who tries to capture him a merry chase.

As long ago as the sixth century B.C. the fox was a featured character in many of the fables told by an Ethiopian slave in Greece who was known as Aesop. The fox's cleverness was so taken for granted that in several fables he is shown as being too clever for his own good, thereby "outfoxing" himself.

Foxes get some notice in the Bible. Samson rounded up

several hundred of them (the Bible does not say how), tied firebrands to their tails and then sent them out to run through and destroy the grain fields of the Philistines. (Of course it was Samson who was being clever in that instance, but one notes that it was foxes he used.) They appear again in the *Song of Solomon* when Solomon refers to the damage they do in vineyards, writing about "the little foxes that spoil the vines, for our vines have tender grapes."

Foxes show their cunning in the fables of India, China, Japan, and other Eastern countries. In Europe, during the Middle Ages, the fox was the crafty, scheming hero of a long tale about Reynard the Fox (or *Renard*, which is the French word for "fox"). The story of Reynard was passed on and added to by word of mouth until finally it became so well-known and popular that it was written down and printed. Through all the twists and turns of the story, Reynard the Fox keeps outwitting one animal after another who tries to bring him to King Lion to be punished for his misdeeds.

Foxes have remained the symbol of slyness and cunning through all the years since. Generals who can confuse and destroy an enemy by quick, darting raids, after which they disappear into some hiding place of their own, are often nicknamed "fox." During the American Revolution, an American brigadier general in South Carolina, named Francis Marion, kept the British troops in the Southern colonies constantly off-balance with unexpected attacks by small parties of armed men. After their surprise raids, they disappeared into the swamp country just as mysteriously as they had appeared. The British general, who tried in vain to capture Marion and his men, finally called Marion "The Swamp Fox."

In the early years of World War II, when the British were fighting German and Italian troops in northern Africa, a German Field Marshal, Erwin Rommel, was so successful in hiding his troops among the dunes and making surprise attacks on the English that he was called "The Desert Fox."

Today, as yesterday, people who have never even seen a fox, except perhaps in a zoo, use his name in everyday talk. When someone does something especially clever or cunning, they say, "That was pretty foxy of you."

How did the fox get such a reputation?

Hunters, farmers, and naturalists tell stories from their own experiences and observations that show the sly fox in action.

One hunter tells of a fox, pursued by hounds, running up a hillside toward the edge of a cliff. He dodged and swerved through bushes and brambles and the hounds followed each dodge and turn. Finally, the fox came to the cliff's edge. There he stopped, in front of some bushes that hid the edge. He stood panting, in full view of the hounds, and waited. They rushed toward him but he held his ground. At the very last moment, he stepped aside. All the hounds, leaping toward him, fell over the cliff to their deaths.

Another hunter has written of a fox, running from some dogs, who rushed into a farm shed. There he leaped onto a shelf too high for the dogs to reach and watched them mill around beneath him. Finally, choosing his moment, he jumped down and, darting past one, jumping over another, made his escape.

But long before the hunt comes to such a pass, the fox has

dozens of ways to throw pursuers off his trail. Dogs or hounds follow the scent of the fox, left in minute particles by his paws on the ground. With their noses down, they chase the scent. Meantime, the fox may run in big loops, doubling back on his own tracks. Now and then he may actually be behind the hounds that are hunting him.

Another way the fox tries to lose pursuers is by jumping into a stream or lake or any other body of water that is handy. The water does not carry his scent. In hilly or rocky country, the fox will make great leaps from rock to rock, causing gaps in the trail he leaves. In farm country he will run along rock walls or along the top rail of a fence.

Another trick a fox uses when he has the chance is to run through a flock of sheep or herd of cattle. His scent becomes lost in the scent of the other animals.

Stories are told of foxes running out onto thin ice and luring the hounds after them so that the heavier pursuers fall through the ice into the water. On the other hand, there is an old German proverb about ice that says, "If it supports a fox it supports a hunter." So there are two points of view about the foxiness of a fox on thin ice. Either way, it seems a fox knows when the ice will support him. (Or her. The females, or vixens, are just as clever as the males, and make use of the same tricks.)

Sometimes the fox tries "playing possum," or acting as if dead, when that seems useful. A farmer, alarmed by a commotion in his chicken house, hurried to the scene and found what seemed like a dead fox lying on the floor. He was mystified but, not knowing what else to do, picked up the limp creature and carried it outside. As soon as he put it

The Fabulous Fox

An old German engraving of a fox "playing possum" to lure crows to him.

down on the ground the "dead" fox leaped to his feet and dashed away.

The same thing happened to a boy who had set a trap in the woods and came to find a beautiful black fox caught in it by the leg and lying dead. The boy was baffled. There were no signs that the fox had put up a struggle and no reason why the snapping of the trap on his leg should have killed him. The boy decided to carry both fox and trap back home to show his family. He laid the fox and trap on the porch floor and called everyone to come see his prize. Then he unsprung the trap. In an instant, that "dead" fox was on his feet, streaking away across the yard and into the woods.

When every other trick has failed, the fox will look for a hiding place. People tell of foxes that hid in chimneys, in kitchen stoves, or in drain pipes. Once a hunted fox surprised a church full of Sunday worshippers by rushing in during the service. Another time a fox, about to be caught by hounds, looked around in vain for any sort of hiding place and then jumped up into the arms of a woman who was standing nearby. Unfortunately, the person who recorded that event did not say what happened next. Did the woman throw the fox to the hounds, or did she take pity on him? Had the fox been foxy, or had he outfoxed himself?

The fox as a hunter is just as cunning as when he is being hunted. Sometimes he "plays possum" to trap prey. He will lie in a field as though dead and curious hawks will circle nearer and nearer, wondering if they have found something for dinner. One hawk circles down for a landing. Snap! the fox has him.

Usually, however, the fox hunts with his nose, following the scent of some small animal or bird that will make a good meal. He always tries to stay downwind from his prey, moving in a direction so that the wind blows his scent away from the creature he is hunting. As he comes close to his prey he begins to move very slowly, wriggling along close to the ground. Then, when he is close enough, he springs. People also have seen foxes doing stiff-legged dances in one spot. This usually happens when a fox has jumped for a mouse in the underbrush and missed on the first try. He dances about to get the mouse running again, and hopes for better luck with the next pounce.

Foxes are clever even in such a matter as ridding themselves of fleas by which they are plagued just as dogs are. One fox-watcher saw a fox, carrying a leaf in his mouth, wade into a pond, going deeper and deeper into the water until only his muzzle was above the surface. With all of his body except his mouth and the leaf submerged, the fox stood for a few minutes. During this time—or so it seemed to the observer—the fleas infesting the fox all traveled to his nose and took refuge on the leaf he held in his mouth. After this, the fox released the leaf and let it go floating away with its cargo of fleas. Then he walked out of the water, shook himself, and went on his way.

Some observers report seeing a fox collecting the wool of sheep which had been pulled off on hedges or fences, and then, with a wad of wool in his mouth, go into the water and wait for the fleas to migrate to the wool. Other stories tell of foxes collecting horsehair or cow hair from hedges and using that material for the same purpose.

And then there was someone who saw a fox break off a teasel bloom (the teasel is a plant somewhat like the cattail with a bloom like a stiff brush) and then brush his tail with the teasel.

Clever, cunning, and a bit of a dandy too? Why not? For along with being quick-witted the fox is a handsome creature with his plumy tail, deep fur, and sharp, pointed ears. So handsome, in fact, that he *has* to be quick-witted and clever to keep ahead of the humans who want his fine fur for themselves.

Fox Facts

FOXES are found in almost every country of the world. (Australia does not have any, nor does New Zealand, Oceania, Madagascar, the Antilles, and a few other islands.) Scientifically, foxes belong to the order Carnivora (meat-eaters) and the family Canidae, the dog family, which includes dogs, wolves, foxes, and jackals. The major genus name is *Vulpes*, the Latin word for "fox."

There are numerous fox species, the more important ones being:

Vulpes fulva—the American red fox
Vulpes vulpes—the European red fox
Urocyron cinereoargenteus—the American gray fox
Vulpes velox—the swift fox
Vulpes macrotis—the kit fox
Alopex lagopus—the Arctic fox

Vulpes chama—the desert or Cape fox of South Africa
Fennecus zerda—the fennec fox of the Sahara Desert
Vulpes corsac—the corsac fox of central Asia

The *American and European red foxes* are very similar and are sometimes considered as one species. They have orange-red fur on their backs, white-tipped tails, white bibs, black-rimmed ears, and black legs. In general, they are the largest of all foxes, three to four feet in length, of which a foot or more is plumy tail. They tend to live on the edges of human habitation, preferring to be near cleared land rather than in the depths of the forest. They like above-ground locations for their dens, as in bluffs, rock ledges, even the base of a hollow tree, so they can keep an eye on the surrounding territory from the entrance. They are hunted for sport and also for their fur. The black fox and the silver fox are color variations within the species. Captured specimens are carefully and selectively bred for their fur. The platinum fox is another variation, developed from the silver fox.

The *gray fox* is a native of North America, the only American fox that can climb trees. He scrambles up the trunk of a tree and leaps from branch to branch, to rob a bird's nest of its eggs or to take refuge from pursuers. Unlike the red fox, he usually burrows into the earth for his den. His fur is blackish-gray, a salt-and-pepper mixture, and his tail has a black tip. Though his fur is not considered as valuable as that of the red or black foxes, he is widely hunted for sport, especially in the southern United States.

The *Arctic fox* is much smaller than the red or gray. His

A young red fox, showing the black-rimmed ears and black legs.

summer coat is gray-brown but changes to snowy white in the winter, a protection against predators in the snowy landscape, and also a heat-conserving color in sub-zero temperatures. His Latin name, *lagopus*, meaning hare-footed, refers to the heavy furring on his paws which enables him to run over the surface of the snow. The Arctic fox has

A blue fox, variant of the Arctic fox.

little fear of humans. Travelers landing at far northern airfields see the foxes along the runways and think they are charming, doglike animals. The personnel at the airfields know them as clever thieves, stealing not only food but bags, gloves, knives, anything bright and colorful that catches their fancy. The so-called blue fox is a variant of the Arctic

The pupils of a fox's eyes are elliptical, unlike those of dogs.

fox. A pup with bluish fur is born from time to time in the litter of an Arctic fox.

The *swift fox* and the *kit fox* are the desert foxes of North America. They are small and speedy but, unlike the red fox and the gray, they are not very wary and so are easily trapped. The kit fox has exceptionally large ears, though the swift fox also has large ears.

The *chama*, the desert fox of South Africa, is sometimes known as the silver jackal because of his silvery gray back.

The *fennec fox* is sandy colored and lives in northern Africa and throughout the Sahara Desert. The fennec fox, too, is noted for enormous ears.

The *corsac* is a small desert fox that is native to central Asia from the Volga River to Mongolia and North China.

He has a thick, warm winter coat and is hunted for his fur, sometimes with falcons. Like the American gray fox, he is a tree climber.

Though foxes belong to the dog family and male foxes are called dog foxes, foxes and dogs never interbreed as wolves and dogs sometimes do.

Foxes have erect, tapered, triangular ears, forty-two teeth, and the pupils of their eyes are elliptical, unlike those of dogs.

Their running speed is not remarkable compared to other animals. Cheetahs have been clocked at seventy miles an hour, lions at fifty, jackrabbits at forty to forty-five. The best speed at which anyone has clocked a fox is about twenty-five miles an hour.

Like dogs, deer, and antelope, foxes are *rotatory runners*. This means that the pattern of their foot movement is left forefoot, left hindfoot, right hindfoot, right forefoot. (In other words, the feet go into action in a circular manner.)

When a male and a female fox hunt together, one generally goes ahead and the other follows, stepping in the tracks of the first. When the pups are taken out for hunting lessons, they too are taught to step in the tracks of their parents.

Foxes are classified as carnivores, or meat-eaters, but actually they will eat almost anything. Depending on the area in which a fox lives, he will eat mice, rats, rabbits, ground birds, snakes, lizards, and fish. He also likes eggs, insects, berries, and fruit. And of course foxes that live near human habitations have won quite a reputation as chicken thieves and bold robbers of duck and goose yards.

The Fox

an old folk song

FOX went out on a chilly night,
Prayed for the moon for to give him light,
For he'd many a mile to go that night
Afore he reached the town-o,
Town-o, town-o,
Many a mile to go that night
Afore he reached the town-o.

He ran till he came to a great big den
Where the ducks and geese were put therein.
"A couple of you will grease my chin
Before I leave this town-o,
Town-o, town-o,
A couple of you will grease my chin
Before I leave this town-o."

He grabbed the gray goose by the neck,
Throwed it up across his back.
He didn't mind the quack, quack, quack,
Or the legs all dangling down-o,
Down-o, down-o,
Or the legs all dangling down-o.

Then old Mother Flipper Flopper jumped out of bed.
Out of the window she popped her head,
Crying, "John, John, the gray goose is gone
And the fox is on the town-o,
Town-o, town-o,
And the fox is on the town-o."

Then John he went to the top of the hill,
Blowed his horn both loud and shrill.
Fox, he said, "I better flee with my kill
Or they'll soon be on my trail-o,
Trail-o, trail-o,
Or they'll soon be on my trail-o."

He ran till he came to his cozy den.
There were the little ones, eight, nine, ten.
They said, "Daddy, better go back again
For it must be a mighty fine town-o,
Town-o, town-o,
For it must be a mighty fine town-o."

Then the fox and his wife without any strife
Cut up the goose with a fork and knife.

The Fox   **15**

They never had such a supper in their life
And the little ones chewed on the bones-o,
Bones-o, bones-o,
And the little ones chewed on the bones.

A Fox Year

GAK! Gak! Gak!"

In a snowy clearing in the woods, high on a Vermont mountainside, two young dog foxes circled around each other, barking and snarling. Not far away, a young vixen was dancing about, yelping as she watched the fighters. The noise that the three foxes made echoed in the cold air.

"Gak! Gak!" The males lunged and dodged.

Then, suddenly, one fox was down on his side on the ground, admitting defeat. The vixen stopped yelping. The victorious male sniffed at the fox on the ground, making sure of his surrender. Then he trotted over to the vixen.

The vixen looked at the victor and whined and fawned. Neither she nor the fox before her paid any attention as the vanquished fox got to his feet and trotted slowly into the woods. By winning the fight, the young dog fox had won the vixen for his mate. So they greeted each other, sniffing and nuzzling. Then they went off in another direction across the clearing.

For the next few weeks the dog fox and the vixen had a pleasant time. They hunted together in the territory the dog fox had claimed as his own, a wide range of eight or nine square miles, part of it second-growth woodland, part of it overgrown meadows long since abandoned by the farmers who had worked them a century before. Far down the hillside, at the very edge of the fox's range, were a few cabins, sometimes inhabited, sometimes not. Now and then the fox and his mate checked the garbage cans and dumps near the cabins to see if anybody was in residence and had thrown out anything tasty. Mostly they stayed on the runways the young dog fox had marked out with his scent, up and down along the ruined stone walls, back and forth in the higher wooded areas. Together they caught rabbits, mice, sometimes a bird, numbed by the cold. When they were lucky and caught more than they needed to eat just then, they dug a hole in the snow and buried the remains, tamping down the snow onto the leftovers with their noses.

Sometimes they played together, chasing each other through the trees or across a meadow. Afterwards, they would find some sheltered spot and huddle together to sleep for a while.

And then some instinct told them both that it was time to look for a den.

The vixen was the one who spied the hole under a projecting rock ledge that faced the south. She nosed down into it. A lingering scent told of a woodchuck who had once lived there, but the woodchuck was long since gone. Inside, the vixen looked around. The den was warm and in good condition. It would not be hard to make it larger.

Now the dog fox and the vixen spent some time each day digging in the den. The vixen scooped out dirt to make the main room larger. The dog dug a new tunnel to make a second exit some distance away from the entrance under the ledge.

Then the vixen began to be fretful, no longer as willing to play as she had been. One day, not quite two months after she and the dog fox had mated, she went into the den and the dog fox knew she did not want him to follow her.

Soon after that, down in the darkness of the den the babies were born, six little pups. They were tiny creatures. The biggest of the litter weighed only four ounces. Their fur was not red like their parents' but grayish brown, and their eyes were closed. They nuzzled close to their mother to nurse.

Outside the den, the dog fox put his nose to the den's opening, heard the faint mewing of the pups and then heard his mate give a small, sharp yap.

Somehow, some way, he knew that meant he was to stay away from her and the babies for a while, and also that it was now his job to bring food to the den for his mate during the time she could not hunt for herself.

He trotted off toward the meadow.

The snow was melting now. Spring was coming. Many more small creatures were beginning to stir in the woods and meadow. Before long the fox was on the scent of a rabbit. He came upon his prey just around a thicket. One leap, and he had the little animal in his mouth and was running back to the den.

He left the food just outside the den so that his mate could come and fetch it when she wanted it. Then he went off to hunt again and find food for himself.

That night he curled up against the bank near the den entrance. He slept lightly, ready to wake at any threat of danger and guard his mate and the pups from any harm.

Actually, the foxes had few enemies in this high wild country. A wildcat might have been dangerous but there was no wildcat living nearby. Humans with their guns and dogs would also be dangerous but through the next days and nights no humans or dogs made their way up the mountainside to the vicinity of the den.

Meantime, the pups were growing bigger and stronger. When they were about two weeks old, their eyes opened. In the darkness of the den they dimly saw the shape of their mother. Dimly, they saw each other. They began to move about, climbing over each other and batting each other with their paws.

A great day came when they were about four weeks old. Their mother began nudging and nosing them up the tunnel toward the outside world. The biggest of the pups was the first to stumble out of the tunnel and blink in the brightness of daylight. It was late afternoon when the vixen brought the babies out for their first glimpse of the big world, but after the den the light seemed dazzling. One by one, four more of the pups came stumbling out. Last of all came the vixen, holding the smallest pup in her teeth by the nape of his neck.

The Fabulous Fox

Red fox pups venture outside the den.

The father fox, sitting nearby, was having his first view of his children. By this time, their gray-brown baby fur had been replaced on their backs by the same sort of coppery red fur as their parents'. If one of the pups had been black, or another had had a black-brown cross on his back, the father would not have been surprised. Red fox litters can vary in their coloring just as children in human families vary in hair and eye color. But all the pups of this litter were coppery red. Their bibs were white. Their boots and their ear tips were black. A fine group of pups—all of them.

Once their eyes were used to the light, the pups found a lot to do. One jumped at a leaf blowing in the wind, another saw a butterfly and scrambled after it. Soon all the pups were playing, jumping at shadows, running after insects, falling over their own feet.

Then their mother nosed them back into the den and their father went off to hunt.

After that, the pups came out to play in front of the den every afternoon. And now the mother began giving them a bit of meat every day. At first she chewed it well before she put it in their mouths. Gradually, she stopped doing that. The pups were growing their own sharp teeth and could chew for themselves.

Summer had come. Trees and bushes and vines were in full leaf. It was time for the pups to begin hunting lessons. One bright day when the whole family was out in front of the den the father fox started off into the woods. He stopped, looked back, gave a "yip," and then went on. The mother fox got up and trotted after him. Then she too looked back and yipped at the pups.

The pups cocked their heads, then one by one, got to their feet and ran after their parents.

The dog fox took his family down a familiar run for the pups' first lesson, a run where he was almost sure to find mice. Suddenly, he dropped into a crouch. The mother

Young red foxes in den

looked back at the pups and her glance stopped them in their tracks. Mother and pups froze while father crept ahead through the brush. After a minute, they heard the rustle of branches, a tiny squeak, and soon the father was returning with a fat mouse in his mouth.

The pups watched carefully, learning from every move their parents made. As their parents moved along, nose to ground, sniffing for scents, so did they. They began to recognize the scents of mouse, rabbit, bird, and snake. As their parents crouched and moved carefully toward some prey, they tried to do the same. At first they made awkward jumps and caught nothing, but gradually they grew more skillful. One pup and then another knew the thrill of catching a mouse all by himself.

Sometimes the foxes came upon a deer or a doe and her fawns. The pups looked curiously at the big creatures and the deer looked back at them. But the father and mother trotted on quietly and the deer went back to their browsing. There was no enmity between deer and fox. In fact, there had been times when the dog or the vixen, running into a herd of deer while out hunting, had romped among them, teasing and chasing, all in fun.

The foxes passed woodchucks, nibbling meadow grass, or raccoons or skunks. But there was no quarrel between these creatures and the foxes either, except in very bad times.

One day, the smallest pup strayed off on his own. He picked up a fresh scent of mouse and crouched to follow the trail. Suddenly he stopped and was very still. Then the mouse darted in front of him. Flip! The young fox hit the mouse with his paw, stunning it.

Pleased with himself, the pup lay in the sun and teased the captured mouse. He let it run a few inches, then scooped it back, tumbled it over, then let it free again for a moment.

He was so busy that he caught no hint of danger to himself.

The hound dog was not ten yards away when the young fox looked up and saw him. The dog was standing, one paw raised, and was whining softly.

In an instant, the young fox was on his feet, whirling to run away. But now the dog was running too.

There was a piercing whistle. A boy's voice called, "Stop, Shep, stop! Here!"

The Fabulous Fox

Some foxes have dens in open fields.

The young fox raced on. It was some time before he realized the dog was no longer following him. He looked back and the dog, and the human too, were nowhere in sight.

The boy, who had called off his dog, was not sure why he had done so. Partly, he had not wanted to see a handsome young fox killed. Also, he had remembered that some foxes carried the disease of rabies. If his dog had caught the fox he might have become infected.

So the young fox was spared. He ran on, not sure of where he was until he heard a familiar "yip."

It was his mother. He ran toward her. She cuffed him,

licked him, and then turned to run toward the den. The young fox ran beside her.

July came and the high-bush blueberries ripened. The foxes lifted their mouths and nipped the berries from the branches. In August, the wild grapes were ripe and the foxes feasted on them. By this time, the pups were practically full grown and all of them could hunt for themselves.

And so it happened that one day the father fox trotted off up the hill and did not return.

A few days later the mother fox also went off hunting on her own and did not come back.

After that, the young foxes also went their separate ways. As autumn came, the foxes who had once been a family ran and slept and hunted alone.

The weather grew colder and they grew thicker fur, their winter pelage. The snow came and each of them had to spend more time hunting because many small creatures were tucked into holes and dens.

With the cold and snow, human hunters came farther up the mountain with their guns. Many of them were hunting deer but they were willing to pick off a fox if they found one.

On a cloudy afternoon, the biggest of the young foxes caught the scent of man in the air. He was very still a moment, and then he began to run in the opposite direction.

Crack! Something whizzed over the young fox's head. He ran faster, swerving between tree trunks. He heard another shot. It was farther away and nothing whizzed by him, but he did not slow down. He ran for a long time before he stopped to sniff the air. The smell of danger was gone.

By midsummer a red fox pup is ready to try hunting on his own.

The place to which he had come was very familiar to him. He was under the bank by the entrance to the den where he had been born. There were still some bones before the den's entrance left over from last summer's feasting. Now he found a sheltered spot against the bank, lay down in the snow, curled his tail around him, and went to sleep.

A few days later, one of his brothers was not so lucky. A hunter's shot caught him between the eyes and killed him instantly. The hunter, pleased with the pelt of a young fox, dragged the body down the mountain.

The weather grew even colder, the snow deeper. And then it was the fate of one of the young female foxes to be caught in a trap. She struggled for a day and a night trying to free her leg before the man who had set the trap visited it and killed her.

Four young foxes were left out of a litter of six. It was a very good average for a fox family.

The snow was still on the ground but the days were growing longer. With the easing of winter, all the foxes on the mountain were filled with restlessness. They began going off in new directions, meeting with foxes they had not seen before. They barked sharply when they came across each other.

"Gak! Gak!" And there was a scuffle or a fight.

Males and females both were looking for mates.

The one female left of the litter born under the bank roamed here and there. Sometimes she stopped and gave a strange howl.

Before long two young males heard her call and came running.

Just as two dog foxes had fought over the young female's mother a year before, these two males fought for this young vixen.

"Yip—yap—gak! gak!" The males went after each other and the young female raced around them, yelping and crying.

Finally one fox went crouching off through the trees. The victor came to the young vixen. They greeted each other and then ran off into the woods together.

The cycle had started over again.

Soon the three males of the litter had found mates. And, as it happened, the mother and father fox of the year before found each other again and they too went through the same pattern as the year before. Some foxes mate for life.

As spring came to the Vermont mountain, a new generation of foxes was born. Tiny and blind, nuzzling their mothers, the fox pups nursed and were cared for by mother and father until the time when they too would be nudged out into the sunshine to play before the den. And then, finally, to learn all the tricks that give their kind their reputation for cunning.

a selection from

Beyond Your Doorstep

by Hal Borland

I find foxes the most interesting animals of all to trail in the snow. The red fox is the most common in the Northeast, though the gray fox is a resident in all but the Plains States and the far Northwest. We have both species where I live and over much of New England. The red fox has a white tip to its tail and is a warm reddish-brown. The gray fox is salt-and-pepper gray and his tail is black-tipped. The tracks of the two are virtually identical. They look very much like the tracks of a large house cat. But if you find a particularly clear print you will see the mark of claws on a fox foot and no claws on a cat foot. Foxes have fixed claws, like a dog's. A cat's claws are retractable. Unlike a dog, a fox walks with one foot almost precisely behind another, so that the tracks make a straight line, not a twin line of staggered prints.

Foxes occasionally come down to my house, as they do to most country places. During the Fall and Winter we often hear them barking in the nearby pasture, and one night one barked directly under the windows of the sleeping porch. His tracks were there the next morning, showing that he had gone around the house, investigated the paths and out-buildings, visited the compost heap, then had returned to his hunting in the pasture. Sometimes I find where a fox has caught a field mouse, a meadow vole, or a cottontail. There may be the marks of a brief struggle by the rabbit, but where a mouse or vole has been killed there are only the marks of the fox's pounce and a tiny drop or two of blood to prove the kill.

The most surprising fox escapade I ever followed out was at the railroad track which crosses my land. It is a stub line on which a short freight train is run every other day, so on odd days the snow lies untouched on the rails. One morning after a four-inch snowfall I found fox tracks between the rails and followed them for a few hundred yards. Then the fox, prankish as a small boy, climbed onto one rail and tried to walk it. The prints were clear as day on the rail, still covered with pristine snow. Mr. Fox walked that rail about twenty yards, then lost his balance and fell off. He climbed back on and that time walked the rail close to a hundred yards before he fell off again. Once more he got back on, and that time he mastered the trick. He walked several hundred yards before he deliberately stepped off—no slip that time—and walked away, apparently satisfied with his skill and tired of the trick. Then I, of course, had to try it myself. I couldn't walk that snow-clad rail more than fifteen yards before I lost my balance.

(Well-known nature writer Hal Borland described his adventures in tracking a fox in his book about country living published in 1962.)

The Fabulous Fox

The Fox Hunt

"VIEW Halloa!"

In the frosty air, the call echoes loud and clear. Across the meadow, twenty or thirty red-coated men and women on horseback look toward the hunter who has called and then spur their mounts to gallop in his direction. The call "View Halloa!" means that the caller has sighted the fox that the hounds are pursuing and now all the field can follow the trail.

"Tally-o!" and "Tally-o-over!" are other cries, meaning "I have seen a fox!" Sometimes the chief huntsman will blow a blast on his horn to further rally the other hunters.

All this—special words, special costumes and customs, along with a whole body of rules and regulations—is part of the formal sport of fox hunting which first began some 250 years ago in England.

Before that time nobody hunted foxes for sport. Foxes were killed because people thought of them as "vermin," a term very like "weed," meaning that foxes were considered small animals bothersome to humans in one way or another. Chiefly, they caught farm fowl, such as chickens, ducks, and geese, as well as pheasants and other wild fowl that people wanted for themselves. And so people trapped foxes, clubbed them, put poison in their holes, and did everything else they could do to exterminate them.

Hunting for sport was generally a pastime for noblemen and they hunted such creatures as the stag or the boar— "noble game." Ordinary people and peasants were forbidden to hunt such game. In fact, they were forbidden to hunt at all on land belonging to the nobility, and since that was most of the land, common people simply did not hunt.

Then, gradually, some of that began to change. In England, especially, there was a growing class of landowners who were not noblemen. Many of them lived on their country estates and did not have much to do except hunt. By this time, "noble game," like stags and boars, was growing scarce, so these country squires hunted hares and pheasants. No one knows who first realized that the fox was an exciting animal to chase. Perhaps one day, some country gentleman who was out hunting saw his dogs distracted by a fox that crossed their path. He followed as his dogs went after the fox and found it good sport. Perhaps he spoke of it to a neighbor and then they went after a fox together. However it happened, it became the fashion for groups of hunters to gather to pursue a fox.

The whole ritual of fox hunting began to take shape.

An English fox-hunting scene in the nineteenth century.

Groups of hunters who came together regularly established "hunts" that were very like clubs, with regular members paying dues and visitors allowed to join in now and then by paying a certain fee. The costume of a black bowler hat and a red coat (often called pink, no one knows why) became the standard outfit for regular members of a hunt. Each hunt hired a Master of the Hounds to coordinate its activities and he had "whippers-in" to assist him. Various English hunts became famous.

American colonists on the eastern seaboard, particularly in Virginia and Maryland, took up the English sport. George Washington liked to ride to the hounds and he was pleased when his French ally, the Marquis de Lafayette, sent him some foxhounds as a gift.

Hounds to hunt foxes were being especially bred by that time—big, deep-chested dogs with powerful hind legs. This was quite a different dog from the fox terrier, originally used to dig after foxes when they hid in their holes or dens. When the chief interest became the chase, the terriers were no longer used in the hunt. The hounds were bred for speed and for "nose," meaning the ability to follow the scent of the fox. Hunters also were interested in the baying of the hounds when they were on the trail. This baying was called "music," and some hunters were more entranced by their hounds' music than their noses. One English hunter was so charmed by the music of his hounds that he had the bells in the local church tuned to echo their cries.

It became the custom to reckon the size of a pack of hounds by "couples." A pack of eighteen couples consists of thirty-six hounds, and a couple can be two males or two females, or one of each. Hound pups, born in winter or early spring, are raised by their mothers to the age of ten weeks or so, and then, depending on the hunt, are sent to neighboring farms to be brought up naturally until time for their training, or to kennels.

Frequently, the pups are marked for identification by the initials of the hunt tattooed in one ear. Another custom is to give all the pups of one litter names beginning with the same letter, or the same second name, as Honey Pye, Raisin Pye, Ginger Pye, and so on.

When the pups are about a year old, or nearly fully grown, their training begins. They are taken out daily and taught to respond to the scent of fox and that scent only, and to follow the trail of the scent. This period of training is

The Fabulous Fox

called "cub hunting" and with it the young hound is "entered" as a working foxhound. The age of a foxhound is reckoned from the year he is "entered." To say "He's a third-season hound" would mean the hound was entered three years previously and was four years old.

Or one might say, *"She's* a third-season hound." Females are equally as good hunters as males. Some hunts may have packs consisting only of females. In the fox-hunting vocabulary the word "dog" is used only to refer to the male hounds and the females are "bitches."

A lot of care is devoted to the hounds of any pack. Even more study is devoted to the ways of the foxes in the territory over which any group hunts. The Master of the Hounds tries to learn the location of all the dens or "earths" of the foxes in the vicinity. He becomes familiar with their favorite runs, and of course he must know the countryside very well, being aware of all its hazards to hunters either on horseback or on foot. He is also responsible for maintaining good relationships with the landowners over whose property the hunt may ride and arranging to make good for any damage that may be done to fences, fields, or crops by the hunt.

Hunters become very knowing about the scent of the fox. They are sure it is best at night and in the early morning, when it is on moist ground and when the ground is warmer than the air. It is bad, or difficult to follow, when the air is warmer than the ground, in bright sunlight, on very dry ground, or during a heavy rainstorm. And, of course, the scent can be lost when it is confused by other scents, as of cattle, horses, men, or the hounds themselves. This is called "foiling."

Some other words in the fox-hunting vocabulary:

Blind country—Areas concealed by leafy trees or bushes, or containing ditches or drains that are hidden.

Bolt—To bolt a fox is to force him out of his den or earth.

Break—A fox is said to break when he leaves a covert.

Cast—An effort by the hounds to recover the scent after a check.

Check—Hounds check when they temporarily lose a fox's scent.

Covert—All woods, unless very large, are called coverts.

Draw—Hounds draw for a fox when they look for him in a covert; the word is also used to describe the area being hunted on a particular day.

Feather—When a hound thinks he has found the scent but is not sure, he will not "speak," but "feather," that is, wave his tail as he pursues a presumed scent.

Field—The members of a hunting group.

Foil—Any smell which obliterates the scent of the fox.

Fresh fox—Any fox seen during the hunt that is not the original fox being hunted.

Hoick! Huic!—Pronounced "Ike" or "Ark," meaning "Hark!"

Mask—A fox's head.

Music—The cry of the hounds.

Muss—When the fox is killed, the hounds are given a chance to muss it.

Speak—The hounds do not bark, they speak.

Tally-o!—A cry meaning "I have seen a fox."

View Halloa!—A yell given when someone sees a fox but the field is not within easy calling distance.

Wind—A hound does not smell a fox, he winds it.

There are, of course, many people who consider fox hunting a cruel and senseless sport. That witty English writer, Oscar Wilde, wrote mockingly of "The English country-gentleman galloping after a fox—the unspeakable in full pursuit of the uneatable."

However, game wardens and conservationists alike say that hunting, within restricted seasons, can serve a useful purpose. Some animal populations tend to increase beyond the ability of the land to support them. A certain amount of hunting thins the population. It is also true that the red fox and the gray fox, the foxes most often hunted, are not endangered species. The San Joaquin kit fox, in the American West, has become endangered, and hunting this fox is prohibited over most of its range.

The number of foxes actually killed by fox hunters is also relatively small. The ceremony of the hunt seems more important to the hunters than running up a score of dead foxes. The horses they ride and their own horsemanship—the way they can jump fences or ditches or follow the hounds on a draw through brambles and brush—are a big part of the excitement. The hounds, and how well or how poorly they draw, check, or cast, their music as they follow the scent of the fox, are also part of the thrill. In most hunts, the fox is just a counter in an elaborate game that tests the skill of humans, horses, and hounds as they pursue him.

Some foxes also seem to find the hunt a stimulating game. There are stories of foxes who are frequently hunted but who refuse to leave their home territory. Sometimes at night

George Washington was a ardent fox hunter and follower of hounds.

a fox will even come near to the hounds' kennels and bark at them as if to taunt them. One hunter tells of seeing a fox and a couple of hounds so addicted to the game that they kept it up long after the human hunters had departed. It was the morning after the hunt, actually, when this man saw the fox walking slowly through the snow, almost too tired to move. Some distance behind him, two hounds, also dead tired, struggled along after him, far too weary to make a dash for him. Why didn't the fox "go to earth," or nip into some hole or den? He seemed as determined as the hounds to play out some ritual of losing them.

There is also the fox who was seen sitting high on a rock ledge, watching with interest as the hounds below him tried to unravel the puzzling trail he had left for them.

In the hilly sections of the southern United States where the gray fox is hunted, a totally different system is followed. There is no riding to the hounds on horseback, no ceremony of wearing "pink coats." On the day, or more frequently, the night of the hunt, the hounds are turned loose to pursue the fox on their own while their owners sit around a hilltop campfire, following the progress of the hunt by the voices of the various hounds. They only leave their cheerful warmth when the sounds indicate that the hounds have captured the fox, or treed him. This is sometimes called "jug-hunting."

When someone goes out alone to track a fox and match wits with him, that is known as "still-hunting." Sometimes three hunters work together, moving in a wide V-formation. The hunter following the fox's tracks is at the point of the V, the other two are ahead of him and some distance apart. As the tracked fox races ahead, the two outlying hunters may get a chance to aim at him. Sometimes the hunter at the point of the V carries a cowbell instead of a gun and clangs it every few steps. The fox is often curious about this sound, which does not seem to spell danger, and comes to investigate.

Luring the fox by sound is a custom that goes back to Indian days, when the Indians called foxes to them by squealing like a mouse. In recent years, mechanical calls, made out of metal, wood, or plastic, that sound like the squeal of a mouse or an injured rabbit, are used by some hunters. And, of course, in this mechanized age, there are even people who hunt foxes from cars, from snowmobiles, or from small airplanes. Hunters who respect the animal they track and follow a certain formal etiquette as they

pursue him disapprove highly of motorized hunting. They
feel such hunting is just mechanized murder and has nothing to do with a game of wits between man and beast.
is every few steps. The fox is often curious about this sound,

Some of the old-time thrill of hounds and horns sounding
in frosty air is reflected in these two poems. The Fielding
selection is the first stanza of a long ballad describing a fox
hunt. John Peel has become famous as a follower of hounds.

A-HUNTING WE WILL GO

The dusky night rides down the sky,
And ushers in the morn;
The hounds all join in glorious cry,
The huntsman winds his horn,
And a-hunting we will go.

—Henry Fielding (1707–1754)

D'YE KEN JOHN PEEL?

D'ye ken John Peel with his coat so gay?
D'ye ken John Peel at the break of day?
D'ye ken John Peel when he's far, far away
With his hounds and his horn in the morning?
'Twas the sound of his horn brought me from my bed,
And the cry of his hounds, which he oft-times led,
For Peel's view-hallo would waken the dead,
Or the fox from his lair in the morning.

—John Woodcock Graves (1795–1886)

The Fabulous Fox

a selection from

Memoirs of a Fox-Hunting Man

by Siegfried Sassoon

THE author relates the experiences of a lonely boy growing up in a small English village in the years before World War I, and the pleasures he discovers in the natural world known to fox hunters. In this excerpt, he is with the stableman, Dixon, who taught him to ride, when he has his first and embarrassing experience of a fox hunt.

Where we rode the winter sunshine was falling warmly into the wood, though the long grass in the shadows was still flaked with frost. A blackbird went scolding away among the undergrowth, and a jay was setting up a clatter in an ivied oak. Some distance off Jack Pitt was shouting "Yoi-over" and tooting his horn in a leisurely sort of style. Then we turned a corner and came upon Denis. He had pulled his pony across the path, and his face wore a glum look which, as I afterwards learned to know, merely signified that, for the moment, he had found nothing worth thinking about. The heavy look lifted as I approached him with a faltering smile, but he nodded at me with blunt solemnity, as if what thoughts he had were elsewhere.

"Morning. So you managed to get here." That was all I got by way of greeting. Somewhat discouraged, I could think of no conversational continuance. But Dixon gave him the respectful touch of the hat due to a 'proper little sportsman' and, more enterprising then I, supplemented the salute with "Bit slow in finding this morning, sir?"

"Won't be too much smell to him when they do. Sun's too bright for that." He had the voice of a boy, but his manner was severely grown-up.

There was a brief silence, and then his whole body seemed to stiffen as he stared fixedly at the undergrowth. Something rustled the dead leaves; not more than ten yards from where we stood, a small russet animal stole out onto the path and stopped for a photographic instant to take a look at us. It was the first time I had ever seen a fox, though I have seen a great many since—both alive and dead. By the time he had slipped out of sight again I had just begun to realize what it was that had looked at me with such human alertness. Why I should have behaved as I did I will not attempt to explain, but when Denis stood up in his stirrups and emitted a shrill "Huick-holler," I felt spontaneously alarmed for the future of the fox.

"Don't do that; they'll catch him!" I exclaimed.

The words were no sooner out of my mouth than I knew I had made another fool of myself. Denis gave me one blank look and galloped off to meet the huntsman, who could already be heard horn-blowing in our direction in a maximum outburst of energy.

"Where'd ye see 'im cross, sir?" he exclaimed, grinning at Denis with his great purple face, as he came hustling along with a few of his hounds at his horse's heels.

Denis indicated the exact spot; a moment later the hounds had hit off the line, and for the next ten or fifteen minutes I was so actively preoccupied with my exertions in following Dixon up and down Park Wood that my indiscretion was temporarily obliterated. I was, in fact, so busy and flurried that I knew nothing of what was happening except that 'our fox' was still running about inside the wood. When he did take to the open he must have slipped away unnoticed, for after we had emerged the hounds feathered dubiously over a few fields and very soon I found myself at a standstill.

Dixon was beside me, and he watched intently the mysterious operations of Jack Pitt, who was trotting across a ploughed field with the pack behind him. Dixon explained that he was 'making a cast.' "He must be a long way ahead of us; they could scarcely speak to him after they took the line out of covert," he commented.

All this was incomprehensible to me, but I was warned by my previous blunder and confined myself to a discreet nod. Dixon then advised me not to wear my cap on the back of my head: I pulled the wretched thing well down over my eyes and made a supreme effort to look like a 'hard man to hounds' . . . I watched the riders who were chatting to one another in sunlit groups; they seemed to be regarding the

The end of a hunt, depicted by a Swedish painter of the last century.

proceedings of Jack Pitt with leisurely indifference.

Denis, as usual, had detached himself from his immediate surroundings, and was keeping an alert eye on the huntsman's head as it bobbed up and down along the far side of a fence. Dixon then made his only reference to my recent misconception of the relationship between foxes and hounds. "Young Mr. Milden won't think much of you if you talk like that. He must have thought you a regular booby!" Flushed and mortified, I promised to be more careful in future. But I knew only too well what a molly-

The Fabulous Fox

coddle I had made of myself in the estimation of the proper little sportsman on whom I had hoped to model myself . . . *"Don't do that; they'll catch him!"* . . . It was too awful to dwell on. Lord Dumborough would be certain to hear about it, and would think worse of me than ever he did of a keeper who left the earths unstopped . . . And even now some very sporting-looking people were glancing at me and laughing to one another about something. What else could they be laughing about except my mollycoddle remark? Denis must have told them, of course. My heart was full of misery . . . Soon afterwards I said in a very small voice, "I think I want to go home now, Tom," . . . On the way home I remembered that Denis didn't even know my name.

(Memoirs of a Fox-Hunting Man *by the British poet and writer, Siegfried Sassoon, was published in 1928 and is considered by many to be a minor classic.)*

Fox Farming

PEOPLE have always worn furs. In the beginning of human history they wore them to keep warm and draped themselves in the hides of whatever available animals they were able to kill. As civilization came along, people began to wear furs for display as well as warmth. Kings, emperors, and czars as well as queens, princesses, noble folk, and rich merchants wore great cloaks of rich furs such as sable, ermine, mink, and, of course, fox. The long-haired pelts of foxes made an extravagantly splendid garment.

The animals whose pelts were used were all caught in the wild state. It was not until 1894 that someone thought of raising foxes in captivity for their furs.

The experiment was made on Prince Edward Island, a province of Canada in the Gulf of St. Lawrence, with two pairs of silver foxes. Soon it was so successful that twenty-five silver fox pelts shipped to London brought an average price of $1,386 each. Such profits encouraged a lot of other people to try their luck at fox farming. Fox ranches sprang up in other parts of Canada, and in Michigan, Maine, and Alaska. This caused the Prince Edward fox farmers to go to great lengths to protect their profitable business. The various men there who had started fox farms agreed together to sell no live silver foxes to anyone off the island. They sent their own fox pelts to England from a post office in New York and got the information on the prices received for them in code. Meantime, as the prices for pelts rose and rose, so did the prices for fox pups. By 1913, the cost of a pair of ranch-bred pups had skyrocketed to as much as $35,000. The outbreak of World War I ended this frenzied speculation in fox fur, and after the war fox farming was resumed on a more reasonable scale. Four brothers named Fromm managed to build up an enormously successful fur farm specializing in platinum foxes in Hamburg, Wisconsin. At the height of its prosperity the Fromm Fox Farm covered more than 13,000 acres and produced more than 12,000 silver foxes a year. Through selective breeding, the Fromm brothers achieved foxes with the lightest, brightest silvery pelts yet seen.

The depression, then World War II, and finally, changes in fur fashion, caused such vast enterprises to close down, but silver and platinum foxes are still bred and raised on ranches in Wisconsin, Minnesota, and Michigan as well as in Canada, Norway, and Sweden.

Among the hazards that fur breeders face is the chance that some pup will be a throwback to some rusty-red ancester. Most unwanted of all by fur breeders is the fox which is called a "Samson." He has underfur but no guard hairs to give his pelt a rich depth. Because he looks "burnt" or "scorched" someone recalled the foxes who were made into living torches by the Biblical Samson and so all these variants have been called "Samson" foxes.

Foxes as Pets

ACCORDING to his biographers, George Washington not only liked to hunt foxes but had a fox as a pet for a while and amused himself now and then by trying to teach him tricks.

In general, foxes do not respond well to such teaching and there are no records as to how Washington's pet reacted. Foxes can become friendly with a trusted human who feeds them but they are usually nervous around people, see no reason to fall in with human notions of how to behave, and are very jealous of their privacy, especially when mating and raising their young. And fond as they may be of food provided by humans, either on purpose or accidentally, they seem to prefer living in the wild.

A foxy smell—a rather mild skunklike odor—is another reason why most people find foxes unsatisfactory as pets.

The Fox's Tail

THE fox's plump tail is one of his outstanding characteristics. As always, people have various theories about its value to the fox. Some have said that the cunning fox uses his plumy tail to wipe out his tracks through snow. On the other hand, there are hunters who believe that so long as the hunted fox is running with his tail horizontal to his body he is still full of energy, but once his tail begins to droop and drag on the ground he is tiring and may soon be caught.

Aesop had a story about a fox and his tail. It was retold by the French fabulist, La Fontaine. This is an English verse translation of La Fontaine's fable, done by Walter Thornbury in the last century.

The fox minus his tail. Engraving by G. Bouget from **Fables of de La Fontaine.**

THE FOX WITHOUT A TAIL

A sly old fox, a foe of geese and rabbits,
Was taken captive in a trap one day
(Just recompense of predatory habits),
And lost his tail before he got away.
He felt ashamed at such a mutilation;
But, cunning as before, proposed a way
To gain companions in his degradation;
And spoke as follows, on a council day;

"Dear brother foxes, what can be the beauty
Or use of things so cumbrous and absurd?
They only sweep the mud up. It's your duty
To cut them off—it is, upon my word!"
"Not bad advice: there *may* be wisdom in it,"
Remarked a sage, "but will you, by-the-by,
Oblige us all by turning round a minute,
Before we give a positive reply?"
You never heard such hurricanes of laughter
As hailed the cropped appearance of the rogue.
Of course, among the foxes, ever after,
Long tails continued very much in vogue.

The fox is also featured in these two fables by Aesop.

THE FOX AND THE GRAPES

A fox saw some fine grapes growing on a huge vine and his
mouth watered for the taste of some. Again and again he
jumped toward the lowest clusters but he could not reach
them. At last, seeing he could not get any however he tried,
he walked away, saying, "Those grapes are sour. I would
not eat them even if I could get them."

*Moral: It is easy to find fault with something one is not able
to attain.*

(This fable is also told with a different moral. During the

German woodcut from a fifteenth-century edition of Aesop's Life and Fables.

Middle Ages, William Caxton decided that the moral of this story was: "He is wise to pretend not to desire the thing which he may not have.")

THE FOX AND THE CRANE

A fox invited a crane to dine with him one day but he offered her only a thin soup in a shallow plate. The crane, with her long beak, could eat nothing and finally the fox licked the plate clean. The crane made no complaint but a few days later she asked the fox to dine with her. She served the food

An etching from Aesop's Fables with His Life, *seventeenth* century.

in a pitcher with a long, narrow neck. The fox could not get his mouth anywhere near the food but the crane easily drained it all with her long beak.

Moral: Sometimes it takes a schemer to outwit a schemer.

an adaptation of

The Wonderful Tar-Baby

by Joel Chandler Harris

AMERICA'S most famous fictional fox is undoubtedly Brer Fox, created by Joel Chandler Harris in his *Uncle Remus* stories, published in 1880. In these stories, just as in *Aesop's Fables,* the fox is always outfoxing himself in his attempts to capture Brer Rabbit.

In this retelling of Brer Fox's most famous attempt to outsmart Brer Rabbit, the heavy dialect in which the original was written has been somewhat modified for modern readers.

The Brer Fox of these stories is the gray fox.

Every evening the little boy came to Uncle Remus' cabin to hear another story. For a long time he had been hearing how Brer Fox tried to catch Brer Rabbit but without success. Then, said Uncle Remus one evening, Brer Fox

". . . and called it a Tar-Baby"

had an idea. He got some tar and mixed it with some turpentine. He shaped this mixture into a body, head, arms, and legs and called it a Tar-Baby.

He put the Tar-Baby at the side of the road and then went off into the bushes to see what would happen. Pretty soon, Brer Rabbit came down the road, *lippity clippity, clippity lippity.* Then Brer Rabbit saw the Tar-Baby and stopped.

"Mornin'," said Brer Rabbit. "Nice weather we're havin'."

Tar-Baby don't say nothin', and Brer Fox, off in the bushes, he lay low.

"You're stuck-up, that's what"

Brer Rabbit asked the Tar-Baby about her health.

Brer Fox, he wink his eye slow, and lay low, and Tar-Baby, she don't say nothing.

Brer Rabbit began to get mad. "What's the matter? Are you deaf or somethin'? If you is I can holler louder."

Tar-Baby stay still, and Brer Fox, he lay low.

"You're stuck-up, that's what," said Brer Rabbit, "and I'm goin' to teach you how to talk to respectable folks. If you don't take off that hat and tell me howdy, I'm goin' to bust you wide open."

Brer Fox sort of chuckle but Tar-Baby don't say anything.

Brer Rabbit asked again for a word from Tar-Baby and

when Tar-Baby still don't say anything he got so mad he made a fist and blip, he hit her on the head. Right there was where he broke his molasses jug. His fist stuck and he couldn't pull loose. The tar held him. But Tar-Baby stayed still, and Brer Fox, he lay low.

"If you don't let me loose I'll knock you again," said Brer Rabbit, and he swung out with his other hand, and that stuck. Tar-Baby still don't say anything and Brer Fox, he lay low.

"Turn me loose or I'll kick the natural stuffing out of you," said Brer Rabbit. But Tar-Baby just held on. So Brer Rabbit lost the use of his feet in the same way. Brer Fox, he lay low. Then Brer Rabbit yelled that if Tar-Baby didn't turn him loose he'd butt her crank-sided. Then he butted, and his head got stuck.

Then Brer Fox came sauntering out of the bushes, looking as innocent as a bird.

"Howdy, Brer Rabbit," he said. "You look sort of stuck up this morning." And after that he rolled on the ground and laughed and laughed till he couldn't laugh no more.

"What happened after that?" asked the little boy. "Did the fox kill and eat the rabbit?"

Uncle Remus said, "Don't make no calculations, honey. Like I been telling you, in those days Brer Rabbit and his family were at the head of the gang when any funny business was going on. So don't wipe your eyes about Brer Rabbit till you see whereabouts Brer Rabbit goin' to fetch up at."

Then Uncle Remus said that after laughing till he couldn't laugh no more Brer Fox told Brer Rabbit that he

". . . laughed and laughed till he couldn't laugh no more"

really had him this time. Nobody had asked him to come strike up an acquaintance with the Tar-Baby and nobody had stuck him fast to the Tar-Baby except himself. There he was, and there he'd stay until Brer Fox fixed up a brush-pile and fired it up so he could barbecue Brer Rabbit.

Brer Rabbit began to talk quite humbly. He didn't care what Brer Fox did to him, he just had one request. "Don't fling me in dat briar-patch," he said.

Brer Fox thought a minute and decided it was too much trouble to light a fire and maybe he had better just hang the rabbit.

"Hang me as high as you please," said Brer Rabbit, "but

"By and by he heard somebody calling him"

for de Lord's sake, don't fling me into dat briar-patch."

Brer Fox thought again. He didn't have any string to hang the rabbit so maybe he'd better drown him.

"Drown me as deep as you please," said Brer Rabbit, "but don't fling me in dat briar-patch."

Brer Fox thought some more. There wasn't any water nearby in which to drown the rabbit. Maybe he'd better skin him.

"Skin me, Brer Fox," said Brer Rabbit. "Snatch out my eyeballs, tear out my ears by de roots, and cut off my legs, but don't, please, don't fling me in dat briar-patch."

Well, Brer Fox wanted to hurt Brer Rabbit just as much as he could, so finally he caught him by his hind legs and flung him right in the middle of the briar-patch. There was quite a commotion when Brer Rabbit struck the bushes, and Brer Fox hung around to see what was going to happen. By and by, he heard somebody calling him, and way up the hill he saw Brer Rabbit sitting cross-legged on a chinquapin log, combing the tar out of his hair with a chip. Then Brer Fox knew that he'd been fooled pretty bad. Brer Rabbit yelled out, "Bred and born in a briar-patch, Brer Fox— bred and born in a briar-patch," and with that he skipped out just as lively as a cricket in the embers.

(Adapted from Uncle Remus: His Songs and Sayings *by Joel Chandler Harris, with the original illustrations by Arthur Burdette Frost.)*

Indians and Foxes

AMERICAN Indians lived in a special relationship with all animals. They hunted and killed the creatures they needed for food, fur, hides, and leather, but they rarely killed more than they required to sustain life. They also had great respect for the animals and asked their pardon, explaining the need that required the deed. They believed that eating some part of the animal one killed would give the eater the characteristic of that creature—the strength of a bear, or the speed of a deer.

Animals figure in many Indian legends, and one tribe, the Hat Creek Indians of northwest America, gave the silver fox credit for creating the world.

Many tribes had a particular animal which they considered sacred and a symbol for themselves. Among the

Muskwaki Indians who lived in what is now central Wisconsin and who were part of the Algonquin family there was one group or clan that had the fox as its symbol. When French explorers and fur trappers came into the territory in the 1600s they called all the Muskwakis *Renards* (French for "fox"), probably because of that one group's emphasis on the fox. As a result, the Muskwakis became generally known to the American settlers who came later as the Fox Indians.

By 1800, the Fox Indians had become allies of the Sacs and lived along the Rock River in northern Illinois. It was a Fox leader named Keokuk who signed a treaty with the white people agreeing that the Fox and Sac tribes would move westward across the Mississippi and leave the eastern banks free for white settlers.

When Black Hawk, a leader of the Sacs, heard about this treaty he was outraged. He rallied the Sacs and a great many Fox Indians as well to remain on the eastern banks of the river and continue planting and hunting there as they had done for years.

The white settlers promptly armed themselves to drive the Sacs and the Fox away by force. Black Hawk and the Indians who followed him were driven to the Mississippi and across it. But the next year Black Hawk fired his followers with new determination. They came back across the river and swooped down on the farms and settlements of the whites. That was the start of Black Hawk's War, a war that terrified the whites so much that they mustered all their strength against the Indians. And, as always when the whites

Keokuk, the Fox tribal chieftain, with his son

The Fabulous Fox

combined forces, the Indians were finally defeated. They left the eastern banks of the Mississippi and retreated westward.

Today, a few groups of Fox Indians still live in Ohio and Oklahoma.

SONG OF THE RED FOX

On that stone ridge I go,
    Hauh, hauh!
East I go,
    Hauh, hauh!
On the white road I go,
Crouching I go,
    Hauh, hauh!
I yelp on the road of stars.
    Hauh, hauh.

—an Indian song
from Northern California

The Feast for the Fox

by Joseph Gaer

A great hound once hunted a fox, but he could never succeed in catching him. At last, after many a long run, the hound decided that the fox was too sly to be caught in an open chase. So he schemed to trap him with cunning.

He went to the fox's cave, and dug a very deep hole at the entrance. He covered the pit neatly with straw and twigs. And upon them he laid out a tempting meal of birds' eggs and wild grapes carefully placed around a young partridge he had killed that morning.

The hound ran off and hid himself near enough to hear what would happen.

The fox returned to his home and saw the feast awaiting him at the door. He sat down and perked up his ears for any sounds. Then he looked at the good food with cunning eyes, and thought:

"It was certainly not there when I left this place. Now, who could have put it there? If a friend wanted to give me all this, he would have brought the gift to me when I was at home. Therefore, this must have been brought to me by an enemy for an evil purpose. It is not safe for me to eat it. It is not even safe for me to remain here much longer."

Though he was very hungry and strongly tempted to taste the wonderful food, the fox softly ran away to find safe lodging for the night.

After the fox had left, a hungry leopard came along who smelt the food before he could even see where it was. He dashed blindly toward it, eager for his meal. But as soon as he stepped upon the twigs and straw, the trap collapsed, and he landed at the bottom of the pit.

The hound heard the commotion and congratulated himself on his success in finally trapping the fox. He leaped out of his hiding place and jumped into the pit, happy his scheme had worked so well.

But when he landed at the bottom of the trap he found before him, not his intended victim, the fox, but his mortal enemy, the fierce leopard. And the hound met the fate he had intended for the fox.

(From The Fables of India *by Joseph Gaer, a book of animal fables intriguingly similar to those of the Western world.)*

The Feast for the Fox   **69**

Fox into Woman

THE belief that human beings could change into the shape of wolves or foxes or some other animal and run about the countryside doing harm was quite common several centuries ago in Europe as well as in China and Japan. This business of changing from human to animal shape later became known as *lycanthropy*. In Europe stories were told about werewolves, or humans who were changed into wolves at the time of the full moon or when under some emotional stress.

A belief in the reverse operation—the transformation of an animal into a human shape—was especially popular in China and Japan, and the fox was usually the animal who made the magical change, generally into the form of a beautiful woman.

According to Chinese and Japanese folklore, there were two ways in which the fox could make this transformation into a human. The legal way was by studying the classic books. Many stories were told about humans who surprised groups of young foxes in a circle around an old white fox who was lecturing on the books that must be learned. The difficulty of this method of shape-shifting was that it took a long time and few foxes had the concentration that it required.

The other method of changing shape was based on foxes making love to humans and so absorbing some of their life essence. There were many stories about beautiful young women who were really foxes seducing young students and sapping their strength till they died. Most of these stories made their way from China to Japan and became part of the folklore there.

The foxes who used sexual trickery were considered criminals and were apt to be destroyed by a blast from the Thunder God. As a result, whenever a thunderstorm threatened, foxes—either in human form or their own— ran for protection to the homes of scholars, who were considered upright men whom the Thunder God would not harm.

Chinese and Japanese folk tales tell of fox revenge, or some ill luck that befell a human who had injured a fox. They also tell of fox rewards, conferred when a human had befriended a fox.

The shape-shifting foxes of China and Japan were supposed to be very fond of wine and were sometimes discovered if they became drunk, for then they assumed their true fox form.

Once, according to legend, a poor man came home and

found his little hut in order and a tasty dinner cooking on the fire. Finally, he learned that every morning a fox came to his hut, shed her skin, and became a woman. The man watched for an opportunity and stole the skin and hid it. For a while, all went well. The man and the fox-woman lived together happily. And then one day, the woman discovered the skin. She put it on, and in an instant her wild nature returned and she ran away, never to return.

Variations of this story are told in countries as remote from China and Japan as Siberia, Greenland, Labrador, and among the Eskimos who live on the shores of the Bering Sea.

The only really good and kind foxes in Japanese folklore are messengers of Inari, the God of Rice, who is himself often pictured as a fox.

Foxes and Cats

ON fox farms, if something happens to the mother of a litter, so that she cannot nurse her kits, the infants are given to a cat to nurse. This seems to work out very well until the young foxes begin to grow their sharp teeth. After that, they must be fed by hand.

That there can be friendship between foxes and cats, particularly between the playful kit fox and a cat, has been observed by various people. The fox and cat romp together and sometimes groom each other.

The Most Delectable History of Reynard the Fox

THE story of Reynard the Fox was the great animal epic of the Middle Ages. The tale traveled from castle to castle, cottage to cottage, and country to country, and often, in the telling, new episodes were invented and added. After printing was invented, the long story was put into print in various different languages, for the tale was familiar and popular all over Europe. This excerpt is from a much later English retelling, edited in 1895 by Joseph Jacobs. The illustrations by W. Frank Calderon are from the same book. A number of animals have complained to King Noble, the Lion, about the crimes Reynard has committed against them or members of their families. The Lion has sent sir Bruin, the bear, to summon Reynard to court to answer for these misdeeds, but Reynard tricked Bruin into getting his head stuck in a hollow log. Bruin has been badly injured in getting free and returned to report his failure to the King.

How the King sent Tibert *the cat*
for Reynard *the Fox*

Then the King called for sir *Tibert*, the cat, and said to him, 'Sir *Tibert*, you shall go to *Reynard*, and say to him the second time, and command him to appear, and answer his offences; for though he be cruel to other beasts, yet to you he is courteous. Assure him if he fail at your first summons, that I will take so severe a course against him and his posterity, that his example shall terrify all offenders.'

Then said *Tibert* the cat, 'My dread Lord, they were my foes which thus advised you, for there is nothing in me that can force him either to come or tarry. I beseech your Majesty to send some one of greater power; I am little and feeble. Besides, if noble sir *Bruin*, that is so strong and mighty, could not enforce him, what will my weakness avail?'

The King replied, 'It is your wisdom, sir *Tibert*, I employ, and not your strength, and many prevail with art, when violence returns with lost labour.'

'Well,' said the cat, 'since it is your pleasure, it must be accomplished; Heaven make my fortune better than my Heart presageth.'

Thus *Tibert* made things in readiness, and went towards *Malepardus* (Reynard's home), and in his journey he saw come flying towards him one of Saint *Martin's* birds, to whom the cat cried aloud, 'Hail, gentle bird, I beseech thee turn thy wings and fly on my right hand.' But the bird turned the contrary way, and flew on his left side; then grew the cat very heavy, for he was wise and skillful in augurism, and knew the sign to be ominous; nevertheless, as many do, he armed himself with better hope, and went

The Most Delectable History of Reynard the Fox 75

The beasts complain about Reynard the Fox at the court of King Noble, the Lion.

The Fabulous Fox

to *Malepardus*, where he found the fox standing before his castle gates, to whom *Tibert* said, 'Health to my fair cousin *Reynard*, so it is that the King by me summons you to the court, in which if you fail or defer time, there is nothing more assured unto you than a cruel and a sudden death.'

The fox answered, 'Welcome, dear cousin *Tibert*, I obey your command, and wish my Lord the King infinite days of happiness, only let me entreat you to rest with me tonight, and take such cheer as my simple house affordeth. To-morrow, as early as you will, we will go towards the court, for I have no kinsman I trust so dearly as yourself. Here was with me the other day the treacherous king sir *Bruin* the bear, who looked upon me with that tyrannous cruelty, that I would not for the wealth of an empire have hazarded my person with him. But, my dear cousin, with you I will go, were a thousand sicknesses upon me.'

Tibert replied, 'You speak like a noble gentleman, and methinks it is best now to go forward, for the moon shines as bright as day.'

'Nay, dear cousin,' said the fox, 'let us take the day before us, so may we encounter with our friends; the night is full of danger and suspicion.'

'Well,' said the cat, 'if it be your pleasure, I am content, what shall we eat?'

Reynard said, 'Truly my store is small, the best I have is a honeycomb, too pleasant and sweet, what think you of it?'

Tibert replied, 'It is meat I little respect, and seldom eat; I had rather have one mouse than all the honey in *Europe*.'

'A mouse,' said *Reynard*, 'why, my dear cousin, here dwelleth a priest hard by, who hath a barn by his house so full of mice that I think half the wains in the parish are not able to bear them.'

'O dear *Reynard,*' quoth the cat, 'do but lead me thither, and make me your servant for ever.'

'Why,' said the fox, 'love you mice so exceedingly?'

'Beyond expression,' quoth the cat; 'why, a mouse is beyond venison or the delicatest cates on princes' tables; therefore conduct me thither, and command my friendship in any matter; had you slain my father, my mother, and all my kin, I would clearly forgive you.'

How Tibert *the Cat was deceived*
by Reynard *the Fox*

Then said *Reynard*, 'Sure you do but jest.'

'No, by my life,' said the cat.

'Well, then,' quoth the fox, 'if you be in earnest, I will so work that this night I will fill your belly.'

'It is not possible,' said the cat.

'Then follow me,' said the fox, 'for I will bring you to the place presently.'

Thus away they went with all speed to the priest's barn, which was well walled about with a mud wall, where but the night before the fox had broken in, and stolen from the priest an exceeding fat hen, at which the priest was so angry, that he had set a gin or snare before the hole to catch him at his next coming, which the false fox knew perfectly, and therefore said to the cat, 'Sir *Tibert*, creep in at this hole, and believe it you shall not tarry a minute's space, but you shall have more mice than you are able to devour. Hark, you may hear how they peep; when your belly is full,

Reynard the Fox welcomes Sir Tibert to his home.

The Most Delectable History of Reynard the Fox   79 come again, and I will stay and await for you here at this hole, that to-morrow we may go together to the court. But, good cousin, stay not too long, for I know my wife will hourly expect us.'

'Then,' said the cat, 'think you I may safely enter in at this hole? These priests are wise, and subtle, and couch their danger so close, that rashness is soon overtaken.'

'Why, cousin *Tibert*,' said the fox, 'I never saw you turn coward before; what, man, fear you a shadow?'

The cat, ashamed at his fear, sprang quickly in at the hole, but was presently caught fast by the neck in the gin, which as soon as the cat felt and perceived, he quickly leaped back again, so that the snare running close together, he was half strangled, so that he began to struggle and cry out and exclaim most piteously.

Reynard stood before the hole and heard all, at which he infinitely rejoiced, and in great scorn said, 'Cousin *Tibert*, love you mice? I hope they be well fed for your sake; knew the priest or Martinet of your feasting, I know them of so good disposition, they would bring you sauce quickly. Methinks you sing at your meat, is that the court fashion? If it be, I would *Isegrim* the wolf were coupled with you, that all my friends might be feasted together.'

But all this while the poor cat was fast, and mewed so piteously, that Martinet leaped out of bed and cried to his people, 'Arise, for the thief is taken that had stolen our hens.'

With these words the priest unfortunately rose up and awaked all in his house, crying, 'The fox is taken, the fox is taken!' and arising, he gave to Jullock his wife an offering candle to light, and then coming first to *Tibert*, he smote him with a great staff, and after him many other, so that the cat received many deadly blows, and the anger of Martinet was so great, that he struck out one of the cat's eyes, which he did to second the priest, thinking at one blow to dash out the cat's brains. But the cat perceiving his death so near him, in a desperate mood he leaped upon the priest, and scratched and tore him in so dread a manner, that the poor priest fell down in a swoon, so that every man left the cat to revive the priest. And whilst they were doing this, the fox returned home to *Malepardus*, for he imagined the cat was past all hope to escape. But the poor cat seeing all his foes busy about the priest, he presently began to gnaw and bite the cord, till he had sheared it quite asunder in the midst. And he leaped out of the hole and went roaring and stumbling, like the bear, to the King's court. But before he got thither, it was fair day, and the sun being risen, he entered the court like the pitifullest beast that ever was beheld; for by the fox's craft his body was beaten and bruised, his bones shivered and broken, one of his eyes lost, and his skin rent and mangled.

This when the King beheld, and saw *Tibert* so pitifully mangled, he grew infinitely angry and took counsel once more how to revenge the injuries upon the fox.

Further Foxes, Flowery and Otherwise

FOXED, *foxing:* Terms used to describe the rusty stains that sometimes appear on the pages of old books.

Fox fire: A phosphorescent glow that sometimes flickers over marshy areas in the darkness. Also, the Japanese call the glow of fireflies "fox fire."

Foxglove: A tall, perennial or biennial plant with long, decorative leaves and purple, yellow, or white flowers in down-drooping clusters. The story behind the name is that these flowers were given to the foxes for gloves by the fairies, for them to wear while stalking through chicken coops at night. The plant is sometimes called fox-bells, and the story behind that name is that in the Middle Ages foxes' tails were considered a charm against sickness and other evils. As a result, foxes were hunted constantly, and finally the animals appealed to the fairies for help. The fairies put these bells through the fields so that they might ring and warn the foxes when hunters were abroad. Scientifically, the foxglove belongs to the genus *Digitalis* and has been used medicinally since ancient times. The Indian tribes of New England knew it as a heart stimulant and it is still used in that capacity today.

Foxhole: A term from World War II for a small, hastily dug pit in which one or two men could seek protection from enemy firing or bombing. Corps Chaplain William Thomas Cummings made the widely quoted remark, "There are no atheists in foxholes."

Foxtail grass: Any grass with a brushlike spike.

Fox-trot: A popular ballroom dance of the 1920s and '30s. Also the international code word for the letter F.

And then there are various creatures who bear some resemblance to the fox:

Fox bat or *flying fox:* A fruit-eating bat of Africa, the Orient, and islands of the southwest Pacific. It has rusty red fur and a foxlike muzzle. Its wingspread is over five feet.

Fox snake: A large, harmless snake of eastern North America. It is light brown in color, marked with blotches of chocolate or black.

Fox sparrow: A large North American sparrow with a bright rusty-red tail. Its breast is also streaked with rusty red.

Fox squirrel: The largest North American tree squirrel, generally rusty red.

Fox terrier: A small, lively dog with V-shaped ears and stubby tail, originally bred to dig foxes out of their holes or dens. When hounds were bred for the chase, terriers were no longer used in hunting the fox.

Finally, there is the word *vulpine*, from the Latin word for fox, *vulpes*, meaning: pertaining to a fox, resembling a fox, or sly and crafty like a fox.

Adages, Quotations, and
Comments on the Fox

WHAT is one to think of this animal, so clever, so quick, and so beautiful? Through the years, writers have recorded their conclusions.

In the seventh century B.C., the Greek Archilochus wrote: "The fox knows many things, but the hedgehog knows one big thing." (The hedgehog can generally escape capture or injury simply by rolling himself up into a ball.)

Twenty-two centuries later, in A.D. 1500, the philosopher Erasmus reworded the same thought. "The fox has many tricks, and the hedgehog only one, but that is the best of all."

Sometime after Archilochus, the Romans had a proverb warning against "setting a fox to guard geese."

In the Middle Ages, the fox tail was part of the motley

costume worn by court jesters and fools, and so the remark, "I gave him a flap with a fox tail," meant "I made a fool of him."

William Shakespeare saw the sly fox when he wrote in *King Henry IV*, Part I:

Suspicion all our lives shall be stuck full of eyes;
for treason is but trusted like the fox.

There is an old saying that "A wise fox will never rob his neighbor's roost."

Another warns that "Every fox must pay his skin to the furrier." (In other words, the crafty are undone by their own wiliness, as Aesop, Reynard, and Joel Chandler Harris, among others, all made clear in fictional form.)

"It was a maxim with Foxey—our revered father, gentlemen—'Always suspect everybody.' " That was Charles Dickens in 1841, in his novel *The Old Curiosity Shop*.

(And that "foxey" father was probably part of the inspiration for a popular comic strip in the early years of the twentieth century which was called "Foxey Grandpa.")

Way back in 1532, the Italian, Niccolo Machiavelli, who wrote one of the first realistic books on how to play power politics, *The Prince*, counseled that "The prince must be a lion, but he must also know how to play the fox."

Is there no one to call the fox "noble," (as stags are often called), or "majestic," like the lion, or "gentle," like the deer, or even "a loyal member of the pack," like a wolf?

It seems not. Quick, clever, and beautiful, the fox teases

us, living on the edge of our lives, stealing from us when it suits his purposes but rarely attacking us. Those who have seen him, head cocked, ears alert, smiling his foxy smile, may feel regret that he has never joined us as some members of the dog family have done, bringing back the sticks that we throw and curling up at our feet. But should we really want to tame and domesticate this creature who is our real link with the wild? Perhaps those of us who live near enough to his haunts to hear him taunt us with his barks at night should be glad that he keeps us on our toes.

Index